The Huckabirds Learn About

Self—Worth

Written & Illustrated by

J. R. Huckaby

FriesenPress

Suite 300 - 990 Fort St
Victoria, BC, V8V 3K2
Canada

www.friesenpress.com

ISBN
978-1-5255-4763-8 (Hardcover)
978-1-5255-4764-5 (Paperback)
978-1-5255-4765-2 (eBook)

1. RELIGION, CHRISTIAN LIFE, FAMILY

Distributed to the trade by The Ingram Book Company

Dedication

To our grandchildren,

Wilson, Reagan and Hollis

and to the grandchildren

yet to be born.

We will love you and pray for you forever,

from earth and Heaven!

Gran & Grizz

Clara And Chloe Huckabird...
Learn to celebrate differences

Mr. and Mrs. Huckabird were so happy!

Their eggs hatched. They had identical twin girls!

They named them Clara and Chloe.

Clara and Chloe were called identical twins because they looked a lot alike. BUT . . . they are not truly identical. Clara and Chloe are each special and unique!

Can you see their differences?

God makes everyone special and unique.

He hopes we will not compare, but instead CELEBRATE our differences! Clara and Chloe were learning to do that.

Clara said, "Good job, Sister!"

And Chloe replied, "Good job, Sister!"

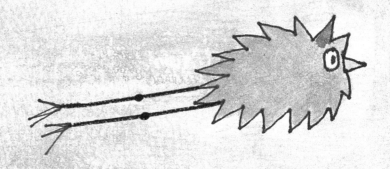

Clara, who had the pink feather, learned to fly first.
She was a really good flier! Mommy and Daddy
were so pleased that Clara had learned to fly.
They chirped,

"Great flying, Clara! Hoorah! Hoorah!
We are proud of you!"

Chloe felt a little sad that her sister was being praised. Chloe was not being praised. Her beak turned upside down. That is what happens when Huckabirds are sad. Being sad about someone else being praised is called jealousy. It can make us unhappy. It can darken our heart a little if we do not let it go.

Have you ever felt sad about another person being celebrated when you were not, like Chloe?

So Chloe made a good choice.

She decided to keep celebrating her
sister even though she did not feel like it.
Chloe chirped, "Good flying, Clara." And
she hoped her time to be praised would
come soon.

Sure enough, the next day the girls were in their nest chirping and singing. It was clear that Chloe, who had the curly feather,

had learned to chirp **very loudly and beautifully.**

Mommy and Daddy heard the girls and chirped,

"Great singing, Chloe! Hoorah! Hoorah!
We are proud of you!"

This time, Clara began to feel
sad and a little jealous. Mommy
and Daddy were not praising
her chirping.

But Clara remembered to let it go. She made a good choice. She celebrated her sister's chirping even when it was a little hard to do. Clara said, "Good chirping, Chloe."

Have you ever made a good choice like Clara did and celebrated a friend or sibling when it felt hard?

Chloe and Clara grew and grew.

They were big enough to go on outings by themselves and be left alone.

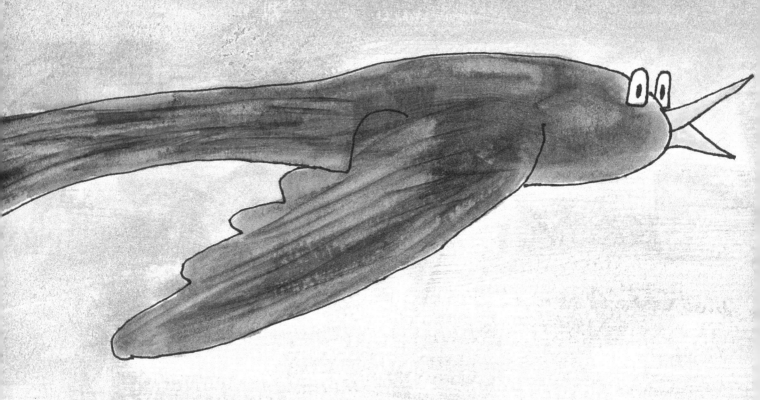

One day, Clara and Chloe were in the nest

by themselves protecting a new egg.

Suddenly, the shadow of an
Egg-Eater bird flew over!

Clara flew to find Daddy Huckabird.

Chloe chirped loudly to call Mommy Huckabird.

Clara and Chloe each used their unique strengths. Mommy and Daddy were able to get back to the nest

just in time to chase away the Egg-Eater bird!

"Hoorah, Chloe for chirping loudly!
Hoorah, Clara for flying fast!"

Mommy and Daddy were so proud of their daughters.

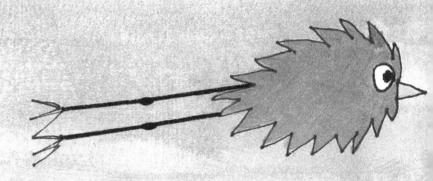

Clara and Chloe saw that day how good it is to be different. We each have strengths. Comparing ourselves to others can make us sad. It can lead to jealousy. They agreed to let jealousy go. Clara and Chloe agreed to keep celebrating each other's strengths.

Can you think of a strength you see in your sister or brother or friend that you want to celebrate or encourage?

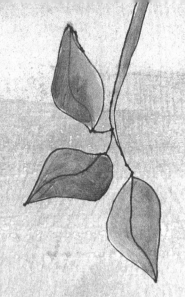

For we are His workmanship,
created in Christ Jesus for good
works, which God prepared
beforehand, that we should
walk in them.

–Ephesians 2:10, ESV

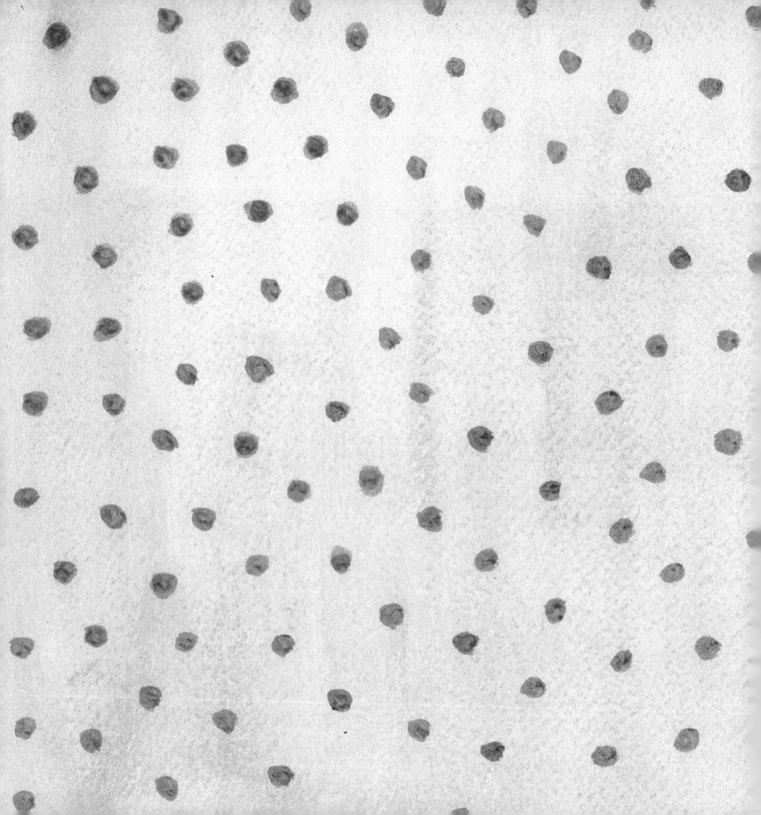

Henry
Huckabird . . .
learns to
avoid the
comparison trap

Hi, I am Henry Huckabird.

I am usually called Happy
Henry, but not after the last
few days!

At the soccer game, Wilson scored four goals. I only scored one. Everyone was celebrating Wilson. They were carrying him on their shoulders! I was sad and felt left out.

(Remember, you can tell when Huckabirds are sad because our beaks turn upside down.)

At school, we had a spelling contest. Ravi got first place, Lucy got second place, and Isla got third place.

I got fourth place, but there was no celebrating or praise for me.

I was even sadder.

Then at home, I heard Mommy praising my sister for making her bed and having her space in the nest all clean. Mommy is prouder of Sister. She is always praising her for being good. Whew, am I ever feeling sad.

Have you ever felt like Henry?

I am flying to Gran and Pop's nest.
Maybe they can help me not feel
so sad.

Gran said, "Henry we are
so, so happy you flew over!"

"Why are you so glum, partner?"
Pop chimed in. (Pop always calls his grandsons partners.)

So I began to explain to them about how Wilson scored four goals and I just scored one at the last soccer game. Then about the spelling contest and how Ravi came in first place and I came in fourth. And then about how Mom is prouder of Sister than me.

Have you ever thought the same as Henry that Mommy or Daddy was prouder of your sister or brother than you?

"Uh-oh," Gran said. "Precious, you fell in the comparison trap! Comparing yourself to others is what has made you sad."

Pop said, "It sure has, partner. Wanting to be better than other birds doesn't make you feel better about yourself. There is enough praise and cheering for everyone! So, if Wilson, Ravi, or Sister is praised, it doesn't take any from you. The more we share praise, the more it grows."

Gran said, "Let me try to help you understand."

Gran said, "Look over the edge of
our nest at my favorite bush below.

It's a hydrangea
and the
beautiful blue
and pink flowers give me joy!"

"But after just a few weeks,

all the blooms turn brown.

My enjoyment is ended."

"But Ms. Anderson, who lives in the big house, learned that if she cut and gave the flowers away,

we actually have more flowers!"

Gran told Henry,

"The more you give hydrangeas away, the more you get! And it is the same with love, praise, and encouragement."

Pop suggested, "Partner, how about you do an experiment? When you go back to school, encourage Ravi for winning the spelling contest. At soccer practice, congratulate Wilson on his four goals. Then tell Sister you are also proud of her. See what happens. Come back and tell us all about it."

Henry agreed to try.

Class Schedule:

10:00 - Spanish
12:00 - Lunch
1:00 - playground

At school, the teacher was putting the schedule on the board while the children arrived.

Henry found Ravi and told him, "Great spelling last week, Ravi. Congratulations on winning!"

Ravi replied, "Thanks, Henry. You are a good speller, too. I was lucky to win. And remember, you won the math contest last month!"

Oh, yeah, thought Henry. I forgot about that! One of my strengths is math. I'm glad I praised Ravi. He reminded me of my strengths. Gran and Pop are right!

There is enough praise to go around!

That afternoon at soccer practice
Henry ran over to Wilson.

"Congratulations on the four goals.
You played a
great game."

Wilson replied, "Hey, Henry,
I was looking for you after the
game—where did you go?"

Henry smiled and thought:
*I guess I went to the comparison
trap, to feel sad.*

Wilson went on, "You scored a great goal. I could not have gotten two of my
goals without your assists! You played a super game!"

Henry smiled at Wilson. He
saw how much better he felt
by sharing praise!

It really did grow!

The next day, Henry was feeling brave and humble.

He admitted to Sister that he wished Mommy was just as proud of both of them.

Henry explained to Sister, "I really don't like making up my bed and cleaning up my nest space."

Sister was so pleased Henry was talking with her. She replied, "I will be happy to help you!"

So they got Henry's bed made and his space all neat.

When Mom saw his clean space AND that Sister and Brother had worked together, she exclaimed,

"Oh, my, I think my heart might burst with joy!

I am so proud of you two working together! I can't wait to tell Dad. He is going to be proud, too!"

Henry flew over to tell Gran and Pop about the experiment.

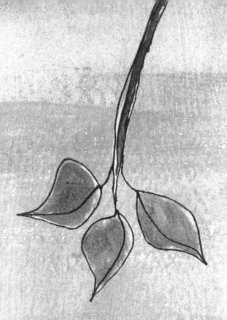

"I did just what you said to do. I praised Ravi for the spelling contest. Then he reminded me that I won the math contest last month. He praised me for that! I also talked to Wilson at soccer practice. He told me he looked for me after the game. He wanted to congratulate me for my goal and two assists! He even said he would not have gotten his goals without the super assists!"

Henry then told Gran and Pop how well things went after talking with Sister. "You were right, Gran, it *is* like your flowers.

The more I praised my friends, the more praise there was! It made all of us feel good!"

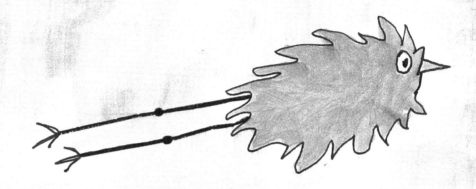

From that day forward, Henry learned that he did not want to compare himself to others anymore and was able to fly over many comparison traps! He decided he liked the way God had made him and he did not need to be better than other birds to feel happy about himself.

Can you think of a time you fell in a comparison trap by comparing yourself? You can also learn with Henry to not compare and to celebrate differences. Agree today that you like the special way God made you!

That night before Gran and Pop went to sleep, they
talked about how proud they were of Henry and Sister.

They were happy Henry was learning not to fall in the comparison trap, but instead to celebrate how God had made each bird unique and special.

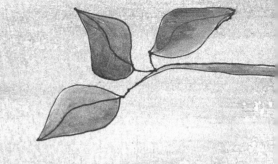

Henry was a great friend to other birds, often giving encouragement and congratulations.

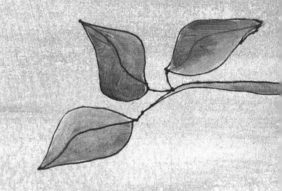

Oh yes, you shaped me first inside, then out
You formed me in my mother's womb.
I thank you, High God—you're breathtaking!
Body and soul, I am marvelously made!

–Psalm 139: 13, 14, The Message

Help For Parents and Caregivers:

Building A Positive And Accurate Sense Of Self-Worth

THE ORIGIN OF SELF-WORTH

You are walking through the National Gallery of Art in Washington and you hear an announcement that a gifted and well-respected contemporary artist and many of her paintings are in the East Building Mezzanine. You and a crowd make your way to the artist and her artwork.

Let me pose a couple questions to you and the other onlookers: Does the artist have value? Does the artwork have value? I would suggest the gathering crowd confirms that both the artist and the artwork have value; however, the artwork was given its worth by the artist. The artwork was nothing more than scattered, unorganized materials before the artist conceived the art in her mind and created it. The artwork now has worth and can be enjoyed—not of its own doing, but of the artist's. This is the core truth of our worth and meaning, as well. We do have value, but it is not of our doing. It is from God. We, too, were unformed substance when God had us in His mind before the foundation of the world. At just the right time, He purposefully knit us together in our mothers' womb—fearfully and wonderfully made we are (Psalm 139). Each one of us is a work of art and we each have a special place in God's kingdom, as well as a unique story and calling (Ephesians 2:10 and Acts 17:26). We cannot conjure up our value any more than the artwork can.

The artwork does not have worth because it was famous and in the National Gallery of Art, but because it was created by an extremely gifted artist. Instead, the Gallery *confirms* a value already bestowed on the artwork. From time to time, the news will report of a painting by a renowned artist that was discovered and sold in Sotheby's auction for a million dollars. The artwork had value whether it was unknown in someone's attic or in a national gallery. Its value came from the artist and the beauty created by the artist.

The illustration is offered as a parable which makes one point. **That point is the foundational truth that we, like the art work, have been bestowed great worth by our Creator-Artist. He created us wonderfully and beautifully, whether we or the world agrees or not.** We are valued by Him and our life story is intended to fit perfectly into His story, uniquely revealing some portion of God, Himself. This is the solid foundation upon which we want to build our children's self-worth. Nothing can ever shatter this.

DOES A SENSE OF SELF-WORTH REALLY MATTER?

At the core of every person there is a self-evaluation, or sense of self, that influences everything. What one concludes about their self-worth will impact every relationship and activity; literally every choice one makes will be influenced. Sometimes we are conscious of it and sometimes not. Regardless of our consciousness, it is a powerful and ever-present force in everyone's life.

The foundational development of this sense of self occurs during our children's early years, under our parental watch. Potentially, this is the most enduring gift we may give to our children—or, sadly, the greatest setback. And as parents and caregivers, we are constantly pushing against the tides of this present culture, tides that are coming from many directions, making it hard to keep our footing. This abstract perception, sense of self, has been given many names over the decades and actually has many facets. My goal will be to offer understanding and wisdom about this powerful perception. It really does not matter what it is called. We will call it *self-worth.* It has been called: self-esteem, self-concept, identity, sense of self, significance, personhood, and other things.

In case you are not yet convinced that *self-worth* is a foundational building block for a healthy soul, consider the importance placed by the following experts.

- *Deeply ensconced in the marrow of our bones is the aspiration for significance. The phrase is abstract but it defines the clamoring beat of every human heart for self-esteem.*[1]
  —R.C. Sproul, theologian

- *Satan's greatest psychological weapon is a gut level feeling of inferiority, inadequacy, and low self-worth. This feeling shackles many Christians in spite of wonderful spiritual experiences and knowledge of God's word. Although they understand their position as sons and daughters of God, they are tied up in knots, bound by terrible feelings of inferiority, and chained to a deep sense of worthlessness.*[2]
  —David Seamands, Christian therapist

- *In my many years of teaching young children, treating families of all economic and social levels, training people from all walks of life, from all the day-to-day experiences of my professional and personal living, I am convinced that the crucial factor in what happens both inside people and between people is the picture of individual worth that each person carries around with him.*[3]
  —Virginia Satir, psychiatric social worker

The question of our self-worth cannot be ignored. Our children will come to a conclusion, whether it is positive or negative. And they will start forming their answers very young—even before they learn to talk. The answer is never totally fixed, but over time it becomes less flexible.

The goal is to answer the question affirmatively and authentically. Until that happens, one is left with an uncomfortable self-consciousness, inferiority, and internal scrambling. When it is affirmatively and authentically answered, one is set free to be other-focused and to be one's best self.

A PRACTICAL LOOK AT THE IMPACT OF SELF-WORTH AS SEEN THROUGH A SEGMENT OF A TRUE-LIFE STORY

I served on an agency board with a woman I will call Marion. She clearly was gifted and wanted to be a help—sounds like an ideal board member. But pause the story and look back to her developmental years. Those years could be summed up by saying she was raised in an unhealthy, dysfunctional family. In order to understand the influencers, here are a few specifics. Though it was an intact family, they were foolish in their parenting. She was often compared with her friendly, compliant sister. Marion heard comments like "she's the one who causes trouble" and was categorized as the "mean one." She was compared and categorized or defined in a lesser position. It was not an egalitarian family—the father had more importance than the mother and the sons more value than the sisters—there was gender comparison. The father also had a bad temper. So it was not an extremely dysfunctional family, but sufficiently so to harm the fragile developing self-worth of a little one.

From her story, we can see some of the influencers that formulate our conclusions. The net effect was that she entered adulthood with the questions of her value answered negatively and therefore felt a gnawing inferiority. Every relational encounter and everything accomplished was an attempt to fill the void of value left by a low self-worth. It was like trying to fill a bucket with a large hole.

Back to the present. Though Marion had been a Christian for over a decade, it was not until the truth of God's love was combined with the tenacious love of friends that the protective, hardened walls of her heart began to soften. Finally, her soul began to embrace the reality that God loved her and had purposely created her, that God said she was very precious to Him even if her earthly father had not. This truth, when embraced, began to slowly quiet the gnawing scrambling inside her from the unsettled question of worth. To show the power of self-worth unresolved and then resolved, I will paint the before and after of serving with her on the board.

Before, team members tiptoed around her. When plans were made there always needed to be special consideration to give her an assignment that was seen as important, and she needed regular assurance that her contributions were really valued. But even with all this energy assuring her, it was just a matter of time before she would be offended.

Her internal clamoring took the form of both *fragileness* and *anger*. But clamoring can have many different looks in different people: *aggressiveness* (demanding, needing the last word), *superiority* (judgmental, having to be right), and *over-sensitivity* (quick to be hurt, extreme timidity). Regardless of the personal style, our uncertainty about our personal value will always manifest itself in unbecoming ways! Some adults are totally naïve about, and unconscious of, this driving force because it is all they have experienced since childhood.

After, Marion finally was able to embrace her self-worth and began serving like she had always desired. Team members no longer tiptoed around her or needed to expend energy with special considerations for her. There was freedom to be focused on the agency's mission and she offered her gifts in greater joy. It was no longer about her. It was about others being helped and God getting the glory. She had far greater joy herself, and the contribution of her time and talents were no longer encumbered by her neediness.

It is now so enjoyable to see her pour herself out, not needing anything in return. She is now one of the most effective people I know to come alongside struggling people and hang in there with them until they, too, can quiet their gnawing senses of inferiority with the reality of God's intimate love and calling. She understands from her own experience that it is often a slow process before the protective walls of our hearts can be broken down and a negative self-worth be replaced by a positive sense of self. She also knows, because of friends who loved her well, that the fertile ground for this growth and healing is in relationships of love and grace.

Let's learn as parents how we can build this positive sense of self in our children from the beginning! We will first look at destructive paths.

THE DESTRUCTIVE PATH: SELF-WORTH DETERMINATION THROUGH COMPARISONS

I do not know to what degree the inclination toward determining worth through comparisons is intrinsic or cultural. Comparisons are at the core of most societal systems: academic, athletic, appearance, marketing, career, economics, religion, and on goes the list. Consider your child's world and the comparison systems she is already experiencing. Try to name the environments in which your child is *free* from value determination by comparison. Can you name any? And even if we somehow avoided the cultural-comparison systems for our children, I am convinced that they (and we) develop internal comparisons, albeit more unconsciously than consciously.

I will use the imagery of pyramids to consider this dynamic of comparison systems, for that is essentially the internal paradigm. As one moves toward the top, worth is gained; as one moves lower in comparison, value is lost.

Approval

Competence

Appearance

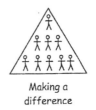
Making a difference

Gain Value

Loose Value

Even the very young child is conscious of comparison, like who runs fastest and who gets the most comments about their beautiful hair. It doesn't take long to figure out the teacher's favorites and who has the best toys. Parents easily fall into the trap getting animated and excited when a child scores a goal one week and paying little attention to the scoreless performance the next week.

Why are comparisons or pyramid systems so destructive?

One reason is it actually is a no-win system. Those at the bottom obviously have their worth wrongly depreciated and those at the top are inclined to think too highly of themselves.

Even for one at the top, there is awareness that the position is tentative. The position comes with disclaiming voices. "Just expand the comparison group a little, and I will no longer be on top of the pyramid." Or: "it's just a matter of time before I'm bumped from this position." Or, another one: "I don't deserve to be here if people really knew."

It is an unfair and exclusive system. Some are born into circumstances that almost place them at the top of the pyramid, while for others, climbing the pyramid seems impossible. It does not offer a healthy path for weaknesses or disabilities, thereby piling on hardship.

Comparison systems pit one against another and are at their core opposed to our greatest longing for our children *to love well*. In a comparison system, another's failure is good because it helps you move up and another's success is bad because it's a hindrance, pressing you lower and diminishing your value.

Pyramid or comparison systems are in conflict with many biblical instructions, like building one another up, rejoicing when others rejoice, or esteeming others more highly than yourself because you believe another's success reduces your value.

Comparison systems create a destructive *scarcity paradigm*—a false perspective that there is not enough value or love or praise for everyone, because only the few at the top deserve the value or praise.

STILL A DESTRUCTIVE PATH: RELIGIOUS COMPARISONS

Often, Christians see the error of these comparison systems and attempt to shift—but, unfortunately, the shift is not far enough. They think they have stepped outside of the culture's destructive system but have actually kept the same system and just tweaked it by changing a few pyramids. The new pyramids are things like "godly character," "noble accomplishments," and "service to others."

I regret that I did not see this more clearly when we were raising our sons. I also regrettably spent a big portion of my personal life stuck in this Christian pyramid system. It is still seeking worth through performance and comparisons, albeit around Christian values, and it still has the exact same downfalls! I have lived much of my life like the older brother in the "Parable of the Prodigal Son" (Luke 15). It is a parable that contrasts two sons, neither of whom is able to enjoy the father's love and presence. The younger brother, more obviously selfish, takes his inheritance and pursues what he thinks will make him happy. The older brother exposes his "comparison system" when the younger brother returns broken and contrite. While the younger brother is away, the older brother has been diligently working to increase his worth through two pyramids— "serving" and "obeying"—and believes, therefore, that he is owed value much greater than his younger brother. But this parable reveals that God has a system that is not ours.

To both brothers, the father's arms are open, and his words are an invitation to intimacy based solely on his love—not what they did or did not do. The older brother is trapped by a sense of *scarcity* that comes with the comparison system. From his perspective, his father's loving response to the younger brother takes away his value or his love. This system says there is not *enough* love and value for both. The older brother's system (despite great values like "serving" and "obedience") is still the destructive pyramid system that has kept him from enjoying intimacy with his father and his humbled younger brother. **The older brother's comparison system crushes his freedom to both receive and give love.**

To see the outcome of religious pyramids just look at the Pharisees. Pyramids like "religious activity," "law keeping," and "knowledge" drive their system. The values are not the problem, but the comparison system is. Jesus calls the self-righteous Pharisees blind fools. Our nature inclines us to be Pharisees and to grow little Pharisees. Even when we understand the comparison system to be destructive, it is hard to leave it. The healthy path is hard. God's path is *humility and surrender.* Many of us have not exchanged our old comparison system for God's system, because the exchange is humbling. We have instead stopped short by assigning the pyramid's spiritual values and kept the same old comparison system.

THE HEALTHY PATH: OPEN SYSTEM

God does not improve or adjust our old systems. Instead, He totally interrupts and calls us to a different realm of living. The *comparison system* is based on performance and outdoing others to earn worth and meaning. In the *open system*, relationships and love give us worth and meaning. There is *scarcity* in the comparison system and *enough* in the open system.

The *open system* foundation begins with God's infinite loving consideration of each of us before the foundation of this world. We existed in the mind of God before our birth. He also gave attentive care to our development in our mothers' wombs and recorded all the days of our lives. His radical thoughtful consideration of us is actually past, present, and future in every minute (Psalm 139).

Beside God's intimate attention to us, He displayed the ultimate extent of His love for us and His desire for us to be in relationship with Him. He loved us when we had no love for Him and sent His only Son, who knew no sin, to be sin on our behalf, that we might be reconciled and in relationship with Him (John 3:16,17 and 2 Corinthians 5:21). For those who receive this gift, they are adopted by God as His own sons and daughters (Romans 8:15, 16). Our relationship with Him is also characterized as that of *friend* (John 15:12–15). We therefore are given worth and meaning by our relationship of beloved children of the King—and not only in relationship with Him, but each other as brothers and sisters.

We are the artwork of the Creator-Artist, and beloved children of the King. We are also purposefully created for specific callings. Each of us is uniquely designed for our assigned good works. We have individually been given distinct gifts to contribute in order to bless and build up others. We are like a body that has many parts, each contributing in order that the whole might flourish. Each has the privilege of playing a vital role in something bigger than itself, which adds richness of meaning and worth to our lives.

This counter-cultural open system gives worth and meaning based upon:

We are eternal artwork of the Creator . . . WORKS OF ART.

We are beloved, adopted children of the King . . . BELOVED CHILDEREN.

We are unique designs for special good works . . . UNIQUE CONTRIBUTION.

We are vital contributors to a Kingdom that will last forever . . . CHERISHED MEMBER.

APPLYING THE OPEN SYSTEM:

Psychologists tell us that the longing of every human is to be loved, to belong, and to contribute. Those longings are fulfilled and experienced in an open system. The foundation of the open system is who God is and His radical attention, love, creation and provision for us, but it does not stop there. As image bearers of the Triune Community, we are also designed to need the love and nurture of others. He has created us to be in meaningful community. Studies show that newborns who are given all the necessities of food and shelter but little nurture will often experience "failure to thrive"—falling behind developmental growth norms. A newborn does not have a framework of reasoning, "am I loved and valued or not," and yet this longing is so powerfully and intrinsically woven into our design that the absence of it affects a little one's whole being destructively. I am convinced it is true in adulthood, too. "Failure to thrive" is no longer measurable in adulthood (except as a medical condition), but it is just as powerful and impactful.

Now how much nurture one needs does vary among individuals. The quantity or quality of succor a person receives from a given relationship and circumstance also varies. Maybe a fair analogy is being filled by food. One person may take twice as much food to be satisfied, based on many variables, and so it seems to be with nurture.

I know adult children from the same family in which one child believes the family of origin was nurturing and confirmed their worth, and another believes there was an absence of nurture and so left the family community feeling little self-worth. How did that happen? It is complex because our needs for nurture differ and there is also the variable of what was intended to be offered not being what was *received*. "We don't see things as they are, we see them as we are" is an insightful truth that is usually attributed to the author, Anaïs Nin. As parents, we are given the most powerful position for answering the questions of worth! And we have to discern as best we can what each child is receiving. It is a sobering privilege.

Additional important influences of peers, coaches, teachers, pastors, etc. will also add voices answering the question of worth. It will be important to foster and protect these relationships. However, you cannot control them. So giving your child a healthy framework for receiving hurts, disappointments, and failures will be integral in this journey. Pointing back to the quote in the preceding paragraph, what an individual tells himself about an interaction or experience has more impact than the event itself. Building the communication pattern of processing disappointments and failures with our child will also be crucial, so that she does healthy things with the memories in her soul.

It will be crucial for you to help your child to develop not only a positive picture, but also an *accurate* perception of himself. Some of the well-intended attempts to help children feel good about themselves are at times counterproductive. If your child could develop the ability to understand and articulate the truth of who God has made him to be, his unique set of strengths *and* weaknesses, your child would have a healthy footing for continued strengthening of his self-worth. The understanding needs to be consistent with their maturity and needs to remain fluid—our children will grow and may mature out of weaknesses. However a godly perspective of weaknesses, both conceptually and specifically, is integral to developing a healthy self-worth. The naïve cultural tendency is not acknowledging weakness and limitation in order to build self-worth, and this backfires. Children will be aware of their weaknesses at some point, and we need to normalize those weaknesses. All people have a unique set of strengths and weaknesses. As a parent, share your weaknesses with your child in an age-appropriate way. Help them see that even those weaknesses are used for good by God.

An *open system* gives **freedom**, since the performance pressure is off.

It fosters **unity**, since comparisons are not needed.

It eliminates the scarcity paradigm created by comparisons—instead there is **enough** love and value for all.

And, lastly, it **unencumbers** one to be God-focused and others-centered, rather than self-focused.

LIVING OUT OF THE OPEN SYSTEM

After a close-up look and consideration of the comparison and the open systems, it seems we would opt for the open system. However, we often do not because it requires humility and surrender that are costly! On some level, we want to believe we *can earn significance* and our *accomplishments can gain meaning*. **Most of us do not have trouble believing we need God's help—we just want God to help us and our children up the pyramid.**

The exchange from the comparison system to the open system begins with a choice of the will to humble oneself. In my innermost being, do I give my heart and mind to my Heavenly Father? Do I surrender my self-reliant attempts to gain value and invite the Spirit to invade all my self-protective walls and prideful attempts (consciously or unconsciously) to be god of my own life? Though the dismantling of the walls and pride is a process, it begins with our will getting out from its "hunkered-down" position and instead being vulnerable before God and others. It requires the decision to hold one's image and reputation loosely and lightly—no small choice. In the case of raising young children, it is fostering humility in them that frees them to believe and receive the amazing worth already bestowed on them. Your capacity to model that others' opinions carry little weight will be significantly important. As parents, we will need to continue the personal work of not falling back in the comparison system.

SO, PRACTICALLY HOW DO WE AVOID THE COMPARISON SYSTEM AND INSTEAD LIVE OUT THE OPEN SYSTEM?

The following are some applications. Each of us will need to develop our own style that is consistent with the personalities and stages of our own family. However, the ideas below can get us thinking about ways to foster a healthy self-worth in our children.

1. Be conscious of affirming and celebrating "being" over "doing." Accomplishments are certainly appropriate to celebrate—but that happens very naturally.

   After a soccer game, celebrate good sportsmanship as highly as goals scored.

   Around the house, try to catch your child being kind or responsible and then celebrate and affirm it.

   At school, affirm leadership and respect for others as much as (if not more than) grades.

2. Be generous with affirmation. A good goal is three positives for any one negative comment.

   Periodically, around the dinner table, take turns highlighting a child and inviting each family member to share what they enjoy or like about him or her. We all need "mirrors" to know what positives others see in us.

   When the children were young we prayed with each one before bedtime. Often, part of the prayer was thanking God for the way He had made that child, the strengths and talents given to him. One night as I finished, my youngest son whispered, "Would you talk to God a little more about me?" We all need encouragement!

As they get older, write notes of encouragement and affirmation on the bathroom mirror.

3. Expose the lie of scarcity   acknowledge there is always enough love, value, and praise for all. One's value does not rob value from another.

   Encourage your children to be happy for a friend or sibling who is being celebrated. Explain to them, in an age-appropriate way, that excitement about another child does not take away any excitement about them.

   When any jealousy is spotted, talk through the lies behind it. Encourage contentment with who God has made her and the plans He has for her.

   Foster the joy of celebrating other's successes. Help our children taste the pleasure in being a part of celebrating another by making a card or baking a cupcake for them.

4. Teach and remind our children the origin of their self-worth.

   There are good resources for reinforcing this truth. An excellent children's book is Max Lucado's, *You Are Special.*

   When our children left the house, instead of a generic "have a good day," we would often say, "Remember, you are a child of the King and belong to our family."

5. Give our children a healthy perspective of strengths and weaknesses, successes and failures.

   There are consequences for successes and failures, **but worth does not change**. For example, if she learns the skills in Taekwondo, then she is awarded the next belt. But if she fails to learn the skills, she doesn't earn the next belt. Make it a point to affirm that she is loved the same with or without a new belt. In children's minds, this all gets lumped together.

If our child is being celebrated for winning the spelling bee, then celebrate fully. But at some point, try to help him consider how he felt when his good friend won the math contest. Remind him we all have different strengths, and that there is room to celebrate *everyone*. The goal is not to minimize a win, but to keep it in a healthy perspective.

As parents, tell our stories of strengths and weaknesses. Normalize weaknesses by acknowledging that everyone is a mixture of strengths and weaknesses. Let our children see us in humility laugh about our weaknesses. (I'm not talking about things that we need to work on as much as areas that we are not gifted in.) An example, I am musically weak. When I sing, most of my notes are flat. So I periodically sing a solo verse of a song for my family and it gets a good laugh. But more importantly, it normalizes weaknesses.

Affirm being "willing to try" over avoiding mistakes and failures.

Teach our children to be hopeful and to have the courage to try new things. In her book *Daring Greatly,* Brené Brown says, "If we're always following our children into the arena, hushing the critics, and assuring their victory, they'll never learn that they have the ability to dare greatly on their own."

IN CONCLUSION

We have trouble not thinking linearly. Our life experience is that we like someone until they do something hurtful to us. But God sees past, present, and future all at once, and He still loves us. He knew everything about you as parents when He intentionally knit your child together in the womb and gave him to you. So work at stopping the comparisons of your child and your parenting.

John Piper wrote, "That's the way we sinners are wired. Compare. Compare. Compare. We crave to know how we stack up in comparison to others. There is some kind of high if we can just find someone less effective than we are. Ouch."[4]

Piper went on to challenge readers to consider Jesus's words to Peter after he compared himself to his friend and fellow disciple John. Jesus had just shared with Peter that he, Peter, would die a hard death. Peter then asked about John's future. And Jesus's reply may feel blunt, but it's also the path of freedom from comparisons (John 21). Jesus says, ". . . what is that to you? Come follow me!"

God chose you as parents (whether by birth or adoption). He knows all. He redeems all. He uses everything for good. And He writes the end of every story. So, lift your eyes from comparing and look to Him. He has given, is giving, and will always give you and your child worth.

Bible References

Psalm 139; Ephesians 2:10; Acts 17:26; Luke 15; John 3:16–18; 2 Corinthians 5:21; Romans 8: 15, 16; John 15: 12-15.

Endnotes

[1] R. C. Sproul. *The Hunger for Significance,* (Phillipsburg, New Jersey: P&R Publishing, 2001), 21.

[2] David Seamands. *Healing for Damaged Emotions* (Colorado Springs: David C. Cook, 2015), 48.

[3] Virginia Satir. *Peoplemaking,* (Palo Alto: Science and Behavior Books, 1971), 21.

[4] John Piper. "What Is That to You? You Follow Me." October 6, 2006. https://www.desiringgod.org/articles/what-is-that-to-you-you-follow-me. Accessed February 6, 2019.

BIBLIOGRAPHY

Brown, Brene. *Daring Greatly.* Avery: An imprint of Penguin Random House, 2012.

Keller, Timothy. *The Prodigal God: Recovering the Heart of the Christian Faith.* Dutton, 2008.

McGee, Robert S. *The Search For Significance.* Rapha Publishing, 1990.

Pratt, Richard L. Jr. *Designed for Dignity: What God Has Made It Possible for You to Be.* P & R Publishing Company, 1993.

Satir, Virginia. *Peoplemaking.* Science and Behavior Books, Inc., 1972.

Sproul, R.C. *The Hunger for Significance.* P & R Publishing Company, 2001.

Tournier, Paul. *The Meaning of Persons.* HarperCollins Publishers, Inc., 1957.